LOOKING
THROUGH TIME

For Terry and Joan
with best wishes

[signature]

Oct-98

OTHER BOOKS

POETRY COLLECTIONS
- The Trophy
- Ghost Country

also:
- A Lethal Kind of Love
  (verse play for voices)

poetry pamphlets:
- Too Wet for the Devil
- The Dinosaurs

FICTION
- The Stars In Their Courses
  (short stories)
- Stories of King Arthur
  (for children)

BIOGRAPHY
- Davies the Ocean:
  Railway King & Coal Tycoon
- John Cowper Powys
  (Seren Border Lines series)

VARIOUS
- Stage Coaches in Wales
- Railways in Wales
- Battles in Wales
- Come Out Wherever You Are
- The Pembrokeshire Coast National Park

LOOKING
THROUGH TIME

HERBERT WILLIAMS

HEADLAND

First published in 1998
by
HEADLAND PUBLICATIONS
Tŷ Coch, Galltegfa, Llanfwrog,
Ruthin, Denbighshire. LL 15 2AR

British Library Cataloguing in Publication Data
A full CIP record for this book is available
from the British Library

ISBN 1 902096 25 8

Printed in Great Britain by
L. Cocker & Co., Berry Street, Liverpool

For Dorothy

I could praise
your joyousness, the way
you are a privilege about the house

And I could sing
your quietude
but you would say that makes you sound too dull

As a wife
you're comradeship for life

and you're a lover
though mother five times over

CONTENTS

IN THE BEGINNING

There was One
and nothing more

He saw the void
it was not good

He dreamed a shape
to fill that void

And thus was born
the Everything

He dreamed of night
He dreamed of day

He dreamed the lion
He dreamed the whale

He dreamed of stars
spun out in space

and last of all
He dreamed of Man

He breathed on dust
to give it life

Too late he saw
what he had done

NIGHT SKY

Nothing in the way.
On clear, incautious nights when clouds
roll back there's
nothing in the way.

They stand out then like stabs
of light, ten
million of them, each
more perilous than words, brimming
with fierce obliquity, skimming
the void that Milton knew.

And then the trekking back
to safe, poised cups
of bedtime coffee,
leaving them there.

The unrequited stars.

SPACES

Spaces come between
people, places, things.
They are the distances
that make us possible.
You, I, he, she.
Space defines us.

Spaces spur actions.
Fists grasp
space as they clutch,
fingers intertwine,
thrusting space away.

Space stitches
the constellations.
Castor to Pollux:
Gemini.

Space is a rivet
joining the ages.
Light years
bind then to now.

INNER SPACE

My inner space.
A dark-lit stage.
The strolling players of the dead
perform there constantly.

I try to change their lines.

They look at me amazed,
not knowing who I am.

TINY SPACE

What comes between
white keys and black?

Tiny space
lets music in.

SPACED OUT

Ironing one day
(like Jimmy Porter's wife)
you cried,
'You never should have married!'

Shouldn't I?
I wondered too,
but knew it to be false, a remedy
for other people's ills.

Now there's no space, but more
an overlapping. Colours blend
around our edges,
making the mix that people recognise.

SCHOOL PHOTOGRAPH
for D.M.W.

I saw you looking out at me

And you knew I was there
oh yes you knew

Although my love for you was not yet born
and you didn't know me from Adam

And all the other faces disappeared
the teachers on their best behaviour
the swots the mischief-makers and the sirens
the butter-wouldn't-melt-in mouths
and soft destroying lips

And only you were left
looking through forty years

and seeing me

NEW JERSEY, '91

We came here in the Fall.
The bright leaves lay upon New Jersey lawns
like promises fulfilled.

So bright they must be blown away
for fear they hurt our sight.

CRYING

Often I have seen you crying
for this, for that,
and sometimes the other.

Your tears have been one long flow
of righteousness.
You have used them
to pay me, persuade me,
and sometimes to betray me.

My angel, the time
for tears has gone.
Make your face
a dry river bed.
We have to go forward.

And you will see
the future arise,
a towering city,
concrete, brass,
rock-dry, bone-hard.

A TALL CITY

Let us make a tall city,
you and I,
a thing of spires and towers.

Let us think high,
reaching up
to the attainable.

The sun will catch its breath,
the moon will glide
around our wishes.

And we will see
Denver on one side,
New York the other.

And we will stand proud,
unconquered,
together.

THE FALL

I see a figure, falling

It is my son, he's
fallen from a bridge,
he hits electric
cables, there's a flash,
a bang!

He is not dead, no,
he is not dead
he is not
he is

He lies
in hospital
smiling
fancying the nurses

It is so everyday
to be alive

We talk about
the food
I bring him
fags
I bring him
books
I switch the telly
on
I switch it
off

And what about
the miracle?

We say the
word
and let it
drop

We are afraid

COMING TO BIRTH

Coming to birth
is pain is terror
leaving warm
safe
torn torn *torn*
awaydown
dark
slip
slip slip slip-
pery
fast
ohstop
nostop
no no nostop
oh!
Oh oh OH!
CHRISTman

allwhite
whitelight
nothinglikelight
no steadybeat
soothing
nosteady
CRUEL!
CRYmouth!
Ah!
AHahAH!

PENTRE IFAN BURIAL CHAMBER

It can be metrically judged:
each stone so high,
so much in width,
weighing so many kilos.
Casting x-long shadows
at y hours on z days.

The whole thing
accurately dated.
No need for guesswork now.

And yet
it is aloof, so far
beyond our reckoning
in every way that matters
that even on summer days
we stand, chilled,
the stones' immeasurable cold
seeping into our bones.

Shivering, we turn
aside. The shadows
move.

THE FIRST IMMIGRANT

He came stealthily
broodingly
every shadow a stranger

His wife yearned for home
fear churning her gut

And what did they find
a land fit for heroes?

The forest gleamed
rivers ran out of Eden

People stared
mouthing a strange tongue

DRAGONS

dragons come at night

grey
     scaly
         dragons

dripping with the dark

crouching
by chimney pots

stoking
their cold breath with
remembered fires

only the mad
can see them

tricked out
in rags

waking
in doorways

staring
with gnawing eyes

BIG ISSUE

human
excrement
bobbing on tide
of commerce
thisgreatcity

scaring the shit

carriers of disease
infection of poverty

scum
waste

even when
they rise
find voices
cry
Big Issue
Big Issue
help the homeless
Big Issue

still
parasites
leeching
taxpayers
shareholders
privately insured
right-thinking

do not
encourage
do not
see
do not
hear
pass them
by

lest we
see
hear
feel
become

sleek cars crunch
gravelled drives
drawbridge tilts up

baron gorges
boar venison swan quail
flings bones to hounds

peasants starve

CALF LOVE

Calf love
is everywhere.

Blue-rinse grans
face riot police.

'Save the calf!'
is the cry.
'Ban veal!'

The homeless shiver.
Two legs short
of pity.

DEPARTMENT X

Department X is where the body lay.
The people came, seeking
a name to give their sorrow to.
They stood awhile then went away
sadly, like stricken dragonflies.

The body lay without a grief to own.
The people came, making
a blame to pin their anger to.
They clenched their fists then went away
coldly, like token elegies.

The body lay. O still as life it lay,
its eyes half-open as in watchful death.

The people came. And then they ceased to come.
Department X was closing down.
What need of it? The war was won,
and all the bodies were accounted for.

They did not know what flag to wrap him in.
He would not tell them. How could they know?
They rolled him up in virgin white,
a bride of Christ, fitting for heaven.

COUNTDOWN TO THE GULF

The more or less accomplices
were mildly stirred to gladness by it all.
The thrill of it, the sense
of drama in the air.

They read the papers eagerly, the rude
tabloids crying war. A new
tyrant was a marvellous invention.
Where else to focus hate, after the thaw?

The trim accountancy began.
X men on this side, Y on that. Z tanks,
and oh, the warplanes! Suddenly
our skies were clear. The jets
that skimmed Plynlimon now skimmed Araby.

Some raised the palm of peace and sent out doves.
The palm soon withered, and the doves
fluttered their tattered wings.
The air was poisoned and they could not breathe.

The careless children played their airy games,
their dark eyes gleaming and their hands
skittering like birds. How could they know
their simple virtue was of no account?

The threadbare politicians spoke,
saying important things. And over all
a silence lay. Complicity
hung like a shroud between the sun and man.

Like shrivelled leaves the spent days shivered down,
till none were left. The branches of the tree
of life were bare. The killing game began.

VE DAY '95

Bands
and booze
Veralynn
wailing
Spamfritters
sizzling
Glenmiller
sounding

War heroes
quarried
picture morgues
plundered

ID cards ration books
ARP helmets
detritus of war
shat out in shopwindows.

Broadcasters
blathering
politicos
posturing

Igniting
of beacons
Queen Mother
in glory

Dresden
Coventry
Stalingrad
Arnhem

Belsen
Auschwitz
pogroms
slavelabour

A day
to remember

A day of
forgetting

MINERS' GALA

They came as conquerors
claiming the city.
Faces proud,
fists clenching marvels:
Ogilvie, Tynant, Onllwyn, Six Bells.
Banners bold
as regimental colours.
Made to endure.

Symbols of unity,
hands joined together,
sickles and hammers,
strength born of oneness.

Queen Street,
Duke Street,
past Bute's castle,
Cardiff was theirs.

In the park
the stuff of dreams —
Nye's visions
bright as the peacocks.

The future is ours!
Grasp it! Hold it!

Who were the conquerors,
who the conquered?
Nye, dumb cast,
breathes not a word.

ON THE BORDER

They were all charm.
A polished pair
from the posh side
of Gloucestershire.

He bought me a drink
and spoke of his son
an officer type
in some damned regiment.
"I'm so awfully
proud of him, y'know."

They were going to Rhaeadr
which she pronounced RADA
as if it were some bloody acting school
then on to Pembrokeshire
which they thought would be quite quaint.

"You know, there's a bleeding tree at Nevern,
a tree that actually bleeds."
She looked at me, eager for response.

"They say it will go on bleeding
till the Welsh get their own prince.
They'll have to wait a long time, won't they?"
She laughed a well-bred little laugh.

"I don't know," I said.
"We're working on it."
She did a double take. "Oh. You're Welsh?"

LOOKING

Looking
in the mirror
for spots
split-ends
small blemishes

Suddenly
she sees
herself
grown old

Putting on
a brave face
she turns aside

The hag
stays
looking out
at lost youth

DREAM MUSIC

(For the pupils of Ysgol Penweddig, formerly Ardwyn, Aberystwyth)

I used to dream
I'd go back to school
with my big band.

There I'd be
all smiles and success
everyone cheering.

The trumpets blew
a gale-force shout.
The roof nearly came off.

And afterwards
the Headmaster said
'Well done, Williams.'

The dream faded.
Big bands died.
Elvis was king.

I knew
I could never compete.
I grew older.

But now here I am.
Not with a band.
No shining trumpets.

Only my words.
Words are dreams.
The music plays on.

CONSEQUENTLY

Consequently
  there are
    times
when we can't
    see
without our
    glasses
(ah yes here
    they are)

When we feel
    lost
the spirit
    wilts
the flesh
    creeps

(he fumbles with his
    script
his glasses
    slide
his face
    drops)

Consequently
  there are
    times
when we feel
    lost
the spirit
    creeps
the flesh
    wilts
the years
    yawn
the grave
    bites

MOUNT CLOUD
(for John Cowper Powys)

In the shadow of Mount Cloud I wept

for myself
my wrongdoing
the state of my soul

for my children
and grandchildren
knowing all that would happen

seeing it plain

with the blackfaced sheep
chomping
the greyfleeced lamb
its neck stained bright
with farmer's blood

SKATING ON THIN ICE

The gulls were skating on thin ice.
Slithering on the lake in some surprise,
wondering if water had been abolished.

The ducks kept safely to the margins,
cruising complacently as ever.
Was the water warmer there, or deeper?

Thin ice comes where we least expect it.
Tomorrow's gulls will wet their feet,
the ducks slither, and poets

will be no wiser than they are today.

THE GOOD OLD HYMNS

Often I can hear my mother singing.
Her voice is still the same. It soars above
the timid efforts of the congregation.
She wasn't one for musical half-measures.

I know just what she liked about the service.
'They sang the good old hymns,' she tells me,
smiling.
It's strange the way she simply hasn't altered.
I never thought that death was so obliging.

The other day I saw my mother walking.
I stopped the car and followed close behind her.
I hurried past and then turned back to greet her.
And found the wizened features of a stranger.

Often I can hear my mother singing,
and so I know that some day I will find her,
I'll sing the good old hymns and see her smiling,
and thank the Lord for being so obliging.

HOW WILL I KNOW YOU?

How will I know you when I find you?
Will you wear a locket, some hair
falling in a way I'll understand?
Or will your tone of voice give me the answer?

It cannot happen yet. For twenty years
you'll grow and then we'll meet.
It may be on the last bus out of Reading,
or on a dusty track in Guatemala.

You have been born again and I will find you.
I'll seek you out as woodworm seeks the rafters.
I'll bring you joy more terrible than cancer.
I'll scourge you for the manner of your dying.

The curious thing is that you will not know me.
I'll be, at best, a crazy old eccentric.
You'll talk about me briefly to your lover,
and then forget my meaningless existence.

THE PLACE I AM

The place I am is not where I would be,
It travels round the earth and far from time.
A miracle is just ahead of me
If I could move away from dusty rhyme.
I would omit the planets and the stars,
And give their orbits to the second-rate,
And be spectator to galactic wars,
And run for safety to the things I hate.
I would be traitor to the noisy blood
That roars unceasing in my troubled brain,
And root out truth from the primeval mud,
And not return till Italy was Spain.

I would be all of this, and something more:
The knock that opens death's amazing door.

FRAGMENTS

I am fragmented.

Pieces fly off me
as if in a gale.

Soon there will be nothing left.

When was I whole?
How did this happen?

FUNERAL ORATION

It's kind of you to come. You're busy people,
and dead men have such shady habits, dragging
workers from their desks and factory benches.
The country really can't afford such gestures.

I shan't delay you long. I simply wish
to thank you for the honour you have done me,
the love you gave me when I was among you,
the trick of laughter and the gift of sorrow.

I loved my wife as rivers love their channels,
I flowed within the confines of her being
not simply out of matrimonial habit,
but in the truth that comes with years of sharing.

I loved my children too. My lovely children.
They grew like trees beside that flowing river,
their shapes and colours changing with the seasons,
their brave roots reaching out to one another.

I had my virtues and my imperfections,
and leave the world no better than I found it.
I'll go to earth as cunning as the foxes,
and let the hunters find another quarry.

ROLL ON THE MILLENNIUM

Barring accidents
we'll be seeing
the new century in

with all its promise
of mass murder
robotic cunning
humanoids

book your seat now
there'll be fireworks

ONWARD, EVER ONWARD

This word processor will be found in a thousand years' time
after the disaster to end all disasters
after the fallout   global warming   ozone depletion
after the unimaginable but wholly expected
after things crawl out from under whatever
after they spawn whatever is in them
this word processor will be found completely undamaged
and I will be sitting in front of it tapping
tapping   tap-tapping   tap-tapping   tap-tapping
tap-tapping   tap-tapping   tap-tapping   tap-tapping

JOURNEYS THROUGH TIME

A sequence of poems commissioned by John Vodden of BBC Wales for his schools radio series 'Wales and the Welsh' and first broadcast in 1978.

> *(Soft, dreamy music)*

Voice One: I climbed a dusty road the other day
because they said it led to heaven knows where,
but time had turned its paradise away,
and all I found were galleries of air.

Voice Two: I sailed my ship upon a summer sea
to find the land of elderberry wine,
but winter blew the promise from the tree
and pressed its devastated heart on mine.

Voice Three: I hitched my wagon to the morning star,
and rode triumphant through the Milky Way,
but when I woke I had not travelled far,
and told my dreams to come another day.

Voice Four: The roads we take are many,
the dreams we find are few,
for tears are two a penny,
and half our lies are true.

> *(Cross fade from music to the sound of a river; faint cries suggesting prehistoric creatures)*

Voice One: The river didn't always flow like this.
They say that once it ran
the wrong way up the valley. Trees were tall

as chimney stacks and fishes flew
like supersonic aircraft. Roses black
as Powell Duffryn brushed the sky,
and cuckoos sang like tenors.

Voice Two: In this time
of strange beginnings man had work to do.
He hacked a knotty hollow from an oak
and sailed upon the water

Voice Three: bearing gifts
for his betrothed
or coals from Aberrhondda.
Who can tell?
The trouble is he learned his craft too well.

*(Cross fade to sound of sea,
becoming increasingly stormy)*

Voice One: The hollow oak became a sturdy craft
that grew a tattered sail
and rode the high adventure of a gale.

Voice Two: At forty knots it clipped the waves
through boundless centuries.
The sirens sang of blameless ecstasies.

Voice Three: And when at last it found its way to shore,
it had become a mighty man o' war.

(Sudden gunfire; the sounds of an old naval battle)

Voice Four: I'm Sailor Joe from Aber Wherever,
(singing)   manning the guns and pumping the hold,
Rougher than rope and not very clever,
My tinder's alight and my baccy is rolled.

I'm Sailor Joe from Aber Wherever,
Cursing the Spaniard, sinking the Frog,
Fighting for King and Country never,
Just for my shipmates and gallons of grog.

I'm Sailor Joe from Aber Wherever,
Splicing the mainbrace, scrubbing the deck,
Drinking and wenching from Rio to Dover,
What's there to do when your life is a wreck.

Voice One:
(pompously)

The Royal Navy's magisterial power
protected trade routes as the Empire grew,
and every day we had our finest hour,
and half the lies we told the world were true.

*(The sound of two or three horses being ridden over
a rough track)*

Voice Four:

The horsemen rode the lonely track
before the sun was born. They passed
the pale, drenched cottages,
the sleeping farms,
and saw the moon skim through the scudding clouds.

Voice Two:

They heard the restless owl, the bark
of skulking foxes, and the heedless wind.

Voice Three:

Their horses dreamed about the stables where
the hay lay warm and tender to the touch.
They whinnied softly in the aching dark.

Voice One:

The horsemen rode the only track
through scrub and moor. The pools
lay cold as virtue in the creeping woods.
The watchful spider waited for the dawn.

(Cross fade from horses to the sound of a wagon train)

Voice Four:	The wagons rolled across the heedless plains.
	The dust rose languid in the smoking air.
	The boulders clutched their shadows to themselves.
	The gullies waited for the winter rains.
Voice Two:	The horses dreamed about the stables where
	the hay lay cool and tender to the touch.
	The women clutched their terrors to themselves.
	The dust lay languid in the smoking air.
Voice Three:	The gullies waited for the winter rain.
	The babies whimpered like abandoned souls.
	Their heedless fathers cursed the crooked sun
	and rode despair through galleries of pain.

(The sound of the wagon train slowly fades)

Voice One:	The horse was always there.
	It was the friend of man
	before the Pyramids
Voice Two:	when Socrates
	was just a shape in the prophetic stars
Voice Three:	when Helen was
	a beauty yet to come, a wistful dream
	of almond blossom in the empty air.
Voice One:	The horse was always there.

(Faint whinnies, occasional stamping of horse in stable)

Voice Four:	I don't know what I'd do without the beast. It's true that he's a drag at times with his infernal stamping and his coat that always needs attention. The old mule is much less trouble and I tell him so, but mules don't really see the point.
	But there, I wouldn't do without the beast. He's pulled my cart a dozen years or more, and soon I'll have to put him out to grass.
	I don't know what it is about the beast. Perhaps the way he nuzzles up to me with such a sorrow in his doleful eyes. I'll miss him when he goes to knacker's yard.
	(Hissing, hooting and clanking of early steam locomotives)
Voice One:	The iron horses came like tinpot miracles, or gods from outer space.
Voice Two:	Turning their hot flanks to the rapid task, lifting their proud heads to the swooning clouds, racing the wind.
Voice Three:	Clanging like coats of armour, ringing like swords, clinging and whining to the shining rails.
Voice One:	Screeching and wailing in the quaking dark.
	(Train noises slowly fade)

Voice Four: We thought they wouldn't last.
The squire was sure.
You mark my words, he said,
they'll blow themselves to Hades.
All that steam
pent up inside, and just the funnel out.
Stands to reason. Mark my words,
the coaches will be back.

But squire was wrong. The railways just got faster,
and folk like me, the stage coachmen of yore,
found other jobs to do, like tending flowers
for daft old girls, or fixing water butts,
or driving four-in-hands on smart occasions.

(Bustle and chatter of crowd, hissing of locomotive)

Voice One: The day the Taff Vale opened
The bells of Cardiff rang,

And all the boys from Ponty
Went down there in a gang.

The band was playing lovely,
The soldiers looked their best

Voice Two: For fashionable gentry
And Lady Charlotte Guest.

The cannon boomed like thunder,
The bishop looked severe,

Voice Three:	He said, 'All this commotion Will wake the dead, I fear.'
	The guard took out his whistle And blew a mighty blast,
Voice Four:	The engine started moving, The bishop was aghast.
	The day the Taff Vale opened The lid flew off the sky.
Voice One:	And all the boys from Ponty drank The pubs of Cardiff dry!
	(Loud cheering, cannon booming, cacophony slowly fading)
Voice Four:	The road's deserted now. The grass claims more of it each year. The dust lies undisturbed through summer afternoons. The wheels turn slowly when they turn at all.
Voice Three:	The inn's deserted too. The cat naps careless in the yard. The rooms are dreary with the burden of the past. The creaking stable slowly fills with dust.
Voice Two: *(singing)*	O time it is a cruel thing And not a friend at all, For lovers who regret the spring Are parted in the Fall.

And time it is a bitter thing
Like days of endless cold,
For joys are past remembering
And all the young grow old.

O time it is a careless thing
And mocks us when we play,
It fills our hearts with reasoning
And takes our love away.

(Eerie music)

Voice One:
(spirit voice)

I've seen it all. The horsemen in the sky
with portents of disaster. Shipwrecks, clash
of chariot wheels in long-forgotten wars.
I've seen the barges on the slow canals,
and patient carters plagued by yelping boys.
I've seen the schooner and the fishing smack,
and heard Columbus scold his sullen crew.

I've seen it all for I was here before
the planets tore their meaning from the stars,
before the tiger and the killer whale,
before the Pharaohs and Pythagoras.

I am the voice of the abandoned hills,
I am the spirit of the brooding seas,
I am the restless wind upon the moor,
I am the crooked dreamer and the damned.

O hear me for I will not come again,
O touch my flowers for they are still in bloom,
O take my hand through paradise and pain,
O feel my presence in an empty room.

For man has made me what I would not be,
A seeker after pleasures still unborn,
He calls me from the bottom of the sea,
And braves my wrath as sailors brave the Horn.

His dark inventions crucify the earth,
He reaps the harvest but he will not sow,
He murders joy before it's given birth
And rides despair through galleries of woe.

(More playful, futuristic music)

Voice Four: I've seen it all, the penny-farthing bike,
the Baby Austin and the Model T.
I've seen them all, the famous and the damned,
but not a beggar gave a thought to me.
And if they say they loved the human race,
I'll tell them they're a liar to their face.

I've seen so much I don't know what to think.
Who rules the planets now we've gone to Mars?
Does time go faster than a giant's blink?
What happens when the Russians reach the stars?

My brain is old, and so's my body too.
I only wish that half my lies were true.

*(Radiophonic workshop sounds indicating
space flight)*

Voice One: Major Green to Ground Control.
The asteroids are out of sight.
We've fixed that trouble in the hold.
The Milky Way looks fine tonight.

Voice Two:	Ground Control to Major Green We sure are glad you're A-OK. But things aren't what they might have been. We calculate it's Judgment Day.
Voice One:	Major Green to God in Heaven. I'm coming in, ten-nine-eight-seven.
Voice Four:	God in heaven to Major Green. I'm checking out. It's not my scene.
Voice One:	Major Green to who knows why. When time runs out we have to die.
Voice Three:	Six-five-four-three-two-one-none Makes Armageddon minus one.

(Space flight sounds rise to climax then
cut out suddenly to give way to absolute silence)